my best friend Fiona

written by **Lucy May**   illustrated by **Kevin Necessary**

edited by **Tasha Stewart**

ISBN: 978-0-578-19708-1

Published by:
E.W. Scripps Company-WCPO
1720 Gilbert Ave.
Cincinnati, OH 45202
Telephone: 513-721-9900
Website: www.wcpo.com

Cincinnati Zoo & Botanical Garden and Fiona are named with permission.
Cincy Shirts' artwork is a trademark of Cincy Shirts and is used with permission.

E.W. Scripps Company-WCPO would like to thank the Cincinnati Zoo & Botanical Garden, Michelle Curley, Skyline Chili, Christopher Schwarz, Michael Perry, Jeff Brogan, Mike Canan, Sue Vonderhaar, Emily Maxwell, Karen Bells, and Josh Sneed and Cincy Shirts for their assistance.

E.W. Scripps Company-WCPO would like to dedicate this book to the memory of Fiona's father, Henry.

Book and cover design: Kevin Necessary, WCPO
Author: Lucy May, WCPO
Editor: Tasha Stewart, WCPO

Thanks to Matt Davies for his advice on doing my first picture book; Tasha and Lucy, for being great partners on this wild adventure; Alyssa Burgei and Mark Schibi at Oxford Physical Therapy for making sure my arm didn't fall off; and, of course, my thanks and love to my wife, Julie, for putting up with me while I painted hippos. — KN

Thank you to Jeff Brogan for the great idea, Mike Canan for the faith we could do it, Dave Niinemets for the moral support, Doug Houston for use of his company credit card and Tasha Stewart and Kevin Necessary for rocking it from Day One. This story is for my husband, Christopher, the most wonderful man I know, and my daughters, Maddy and Katy, the offspring I love even more than Fiona. — LM

First edition, 2017
Second printing, 2017
Printed by Signature Book Printing, Gaithersburg, MD

Hi! I'm Trixie the Tilapia. I live in Hippo Cove at the Cincinnati Zoo & Botanical Garden.

My best friend is a spunky baby hippo named Fiona. Maybe you've heard of her?

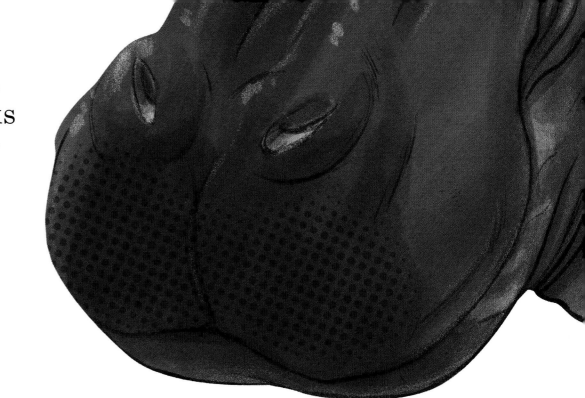

Fiona was born on Jan. 24, 2017, but she was six weeks too early and weighed only 29 pounds.

That would be GIANT for a baby tilapia! But it's only about half as big as a newborn baby hippo is supposed to be.

She was so little
the zookeepers
weren't sure she
would survive.
But they took
care of her all
day and all
night.

Nurses from Cincinnati
Children's Hospital even
came to the zoo to help.

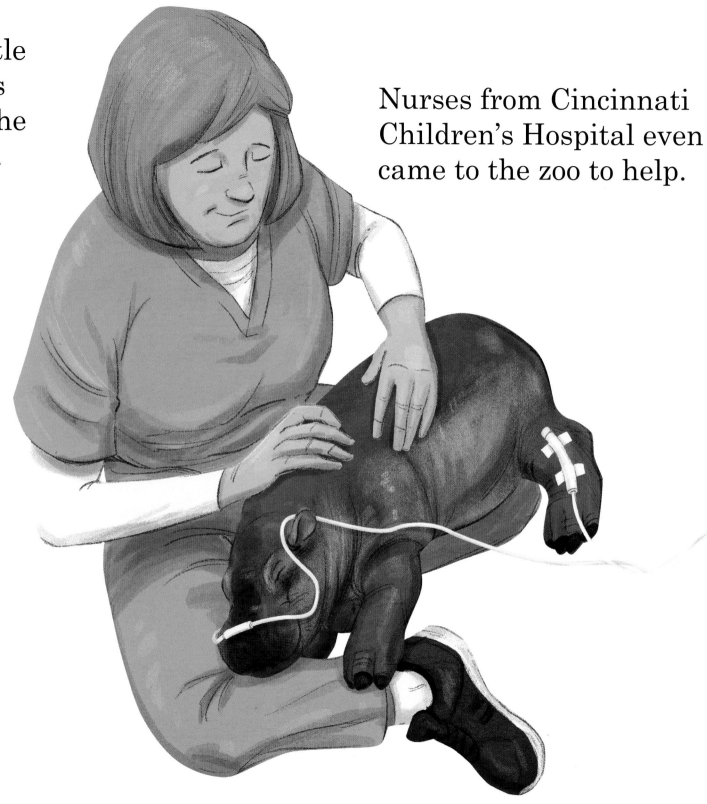

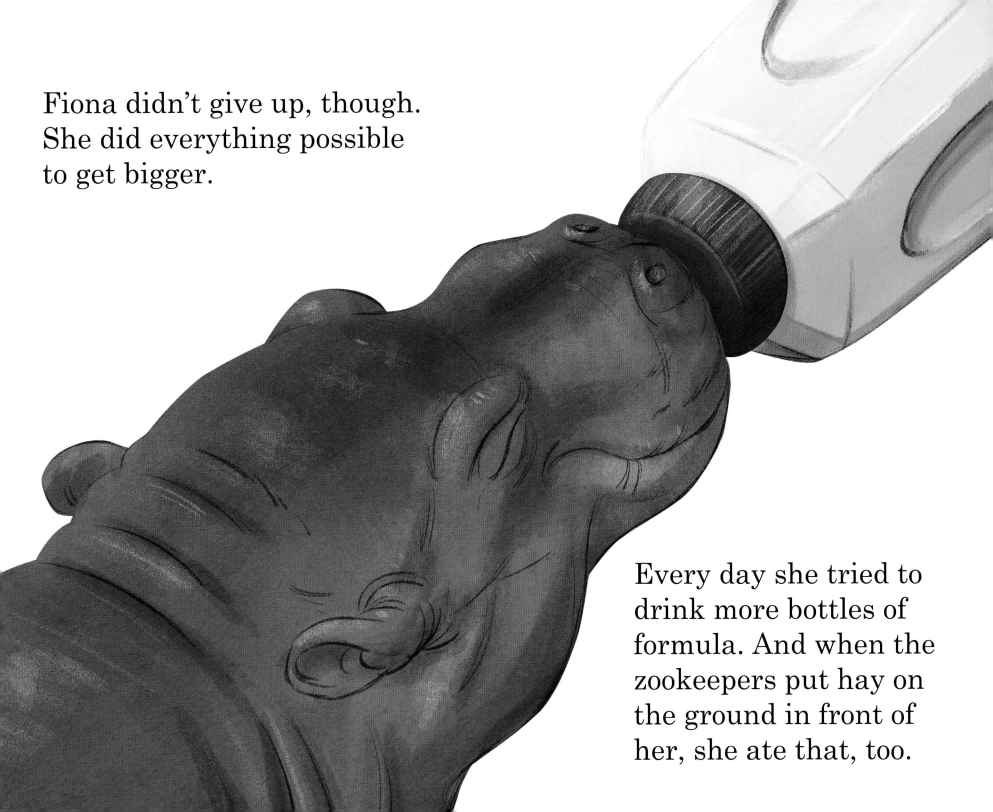

Fiona didn't give up, though. She did everything possible to get bigger.

Every day she tried to drink more bottles of formula. And when the zookeepers put hay on the ground in front of her, she ate that, too.

When she was strong enough, the zookeepers took Fiona to a small pool. She was scared at first, but soon she was playing in the water with her human friends.

Fiona was getting bigger.

And bigger …

And BIGGER!

FINALLY she was big enough to come swim in the Hippo Cove pool with me!

Fiona likes to bounce from the bottom of the pool to the top of the water. It might look like she's showing off. But she has to do that to get enough breath to play with me.

Even though Fiona is big, her mom, Bibi, and her dad, Henry, are both MUCH bigger than she is.

Fiona loves to play with her mom. Bibi lets Fiona look in her giant hippo mouth. Fiona gets so curious that she almost climbs inside!

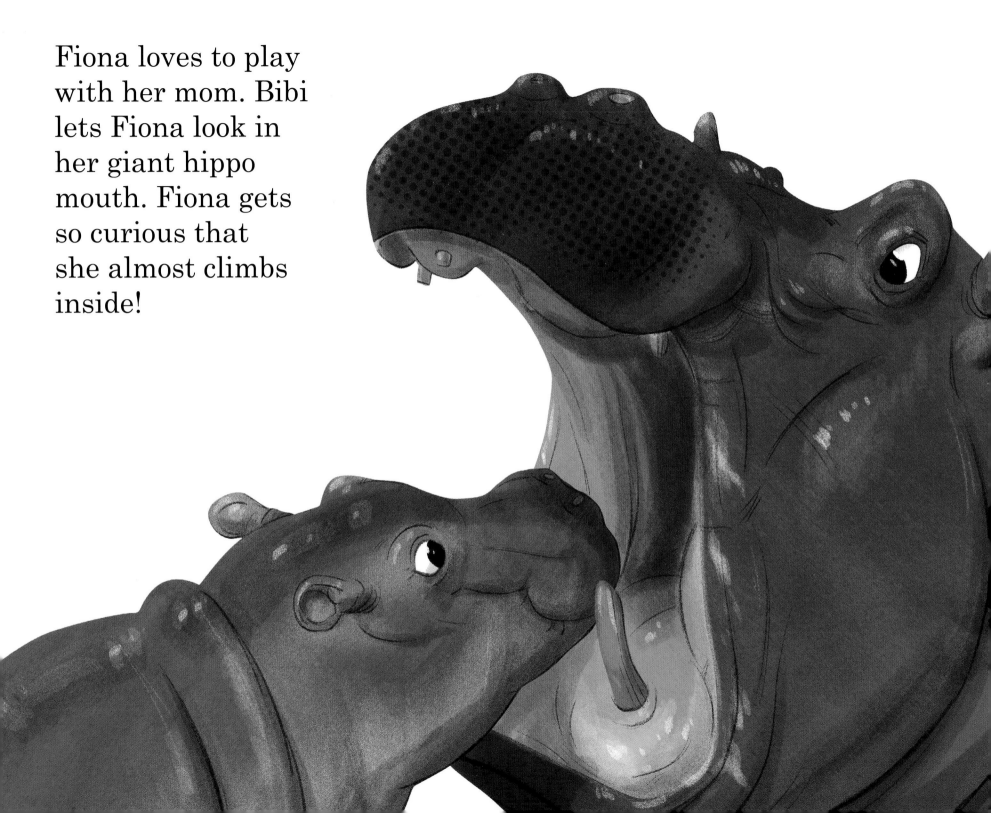

Sometimes Fiona tries to eat her mom and dad's food.

Sometimes she tries to bite
their butts.

They tell her to stop, but Fiona just can't. They love her anyway, though.

Everybody loves Fiona.

People have made cookies and T-shirts with her picture on them. The local sheriff even made her an honorary deputy.

Hamilton County Sheriff's Office

HEREBY NAMES THE FOLLOWING

FIONA the HIPPO

HONORARY DEPUTY SHERIFF

Sometimes I wonder if all of that has made Fiona a little too confident.

Some of the other animals are jealous of all the attention Fiona gets, but not me!

At first I liked Fiona
mostly for her poop
and dead skin. It
might sound gross to
you, but I eat that stuff
to help keep the pool
clean. It's my special
job at Hippo Cove.

Now I like her for
other reasons, too.

She's strong.

She's sassy.

And she never gave up, even when she was very, very sick.

Everyone who comes to visit Fiona smiles when they see her.

Even though we don't look much alike, Fiona and I have a lot in common.

We both love to play in the big pool at Hippo Cove.

And sometimes, Fiona
eats hippo poop, too!

The end.

For coloring pages,
downloadable paper figures,
videos and more, visit

www.mybestfriendfiona.com

About the author

Lucy May is a digital reporter for WCPO and a native of Greater Cincinnati. She has been a Fiona fanatic since the day the baby hippo was born.

About the illustrator

Kevin Necessary is the digital cartoonist for WCPO. He is the illustrator of *Childhood Saved*, a comics journalism series on which he collaborated with Lucy May.

Photos by Emily Maxwell

sponsored by